PMA Positive Mental Attitude:

Ten Ways to Develop and Increase Your Positive Mindset

By

Paul G. Brodie

PMA Positive Mental Attitude: Ten Ways to Develop and Increase Your Positive Mindset

This book is dedicated to my mom, Barbara "Mama" Brodie. Without her support and motivation (and incredible cooking) I would literally not be here today

Table of Contents

Free Audiobook Offer

Are you a fan of audiobooks? I would like to offer you the audiobook of Motivation 101 for free. All you need to do is go to my website at www.BrodieEDU.com/freeaudiobook and provide your e mail address in exchange for the free digital download. The audiobook will only be available on the website for a limited time as I offer free goodies to my readership on a regular basis.

PMA Seminar Invitation

I want to invite you to help bring me to your organization or campus event. Each of the self-help books (Motivation 101, Positivity Attracts, The Pursuit of Happiness, and Just Do It) that I have published are based on my motivational seminars.

These motivation seminars are interactive and enjoyable for all attendees, while also providing invaluable information to employees, students, faculty, and staff of universities.

The intention of the seminars is to help the audience become their greatest champion, improve motivation, increase positive thinking and happiness, and help the audience on the journey to achieving their dreams and goals.

Contact me at Brodie@BrodieConsultingGroup.com with any questions.

Check out this brief video at www.YouTube.com/BrodieEDU to see why you should consider bringing Paul to your organization or campus.

Foreword by Schreese Fontaine

I first met Paul back in 2006 when I was working at Enterprise Rent a Car. Paul was a newly appointed Assistant Manager after our previous manager was promoted. I knew of Paul previously as he had the reputation as one of the top Management Trainees at Enterprise. Paul was also well known as someone who took pride in the mentorship program at Enterprise and served as a mentor for many up and coming trainees prior to him becoming an assistant manager. I got to witness this first hand when we started to work together.

We quickly bonded over movies, music, jokes and being the underdogs of the world. Paul became like my older brother. We had a close bond as Paul make it a point to see the best in everyone, no matter their flaws. Paul has always been a great friend and someone who always encouraged me.

I don't know if you have any experience with Enterprise, but their training program is great to learn sales and customer service, especially as a post college career. The schedule and environment can be challenging with 50 hour work weeks, studying to become a manager, running from place to place all over town to pick up customers, and washing cars in full suits come rain, sleet or shine.

We do it all while wearing a smile and with the goal to give the best customer service experience possible. Our branch was located on the west side of Fort Worth and had quite a few challenges. One of the challenges was the other Assistant Manager quitting soon after Paul started. Our branch was also considered one of the worst in the region.

Paul found this to be unacceptable and empowered me to serve as his assistant. Our branch had three components; the main branch, the satellite branch at Caliber Collision, and also our arrangement to rent cars to Carswell Airforce Base. Paul took over running our branch and I was his primary assistant. We had a small team; the Branch Manager, Asst. Manager - Paul, 2 other management trainees, 2 car preps who cleaned out the cars when returned by customers, and myself.

I was responsible for mapping our day and what reservations to care of. Paul would handle who would be manning the branch and satellite. We eventually grew the branch and it became the only branch to be acknowledged by our main client at Caliber for all the improvements we made. Paul made it his personal mission to make sure we always have enough cars to meet the obligations of our satellite branch located inside Caliber Collision for all the Geico insurance drop offs.

This was an issue in the past and was a main point of contention with the boss at Caliber. Paul went to the area manager about the issue and had him guarantee that we would always have cars for the Geico customers. I remember that during one region managers meeting, Paul called the area manager and told him we needed cars desperately for three customers who were waiting for rental cars. Somehow Paul was able to have three branch managers drive over their own car rentals to the branch for the customers. It was something I have never seen before and Paul's commitment to Caliber helped save the relationship between Caliber and Enterprise. He always made sure that every Geico customer got a car and would typically have them in a car that was ready to go and have all paperwork completed within ten minutes. He staked his personal reputation with Caliber and backed up everything he said he would do.

After the success of the branch Paul had an opportunity to move on to another field in nurse recruiting before he left the corporate world for teaching. When Paul gave notice he was leaving the rest of our whole branch quickly followed within three weeks resulting in the entire branch moving on to new opportunities.

I wanted to share this story because eleven years later I am still in contact with him. Paul always shares his positive attitude even when things aren't going well. He always encourages those he helps to see the bright side and what is ahead. Today, I still consider Paul my big brother. He is still my greatest champion and I can say that part of my success has been having Paul in my corner all these years. I hope that you enjoy reading PMA and I challenge you to believe in yourself and start living your life to the fullest!

Schreese Fontaine

Travel Agent

Irving, TX

Introduction

Welcome to PMA: Positive Mental Attitude. My intention with this book is to help develop and increase your positive mindset. We will cover ten different ways that you can both develop and increase your positive mindset through a variety of techniques and concepts.

One of the biggest challenges in our lives is the ability to not only be positive, but to be positive on a *consistent* basis. There is a lot of negativity that we must consistently battle throughout our lives. I will provide you with the necessary tools to take charge and increase your positive mindset. In 2008, I created the PMA seminar with the intention of helping people shift their focus to the positive aspects of their lives.

Chapter 1 What is PMA? I provide an explanation of how I created the PMA seminar in September 2008. PMA is an acronym for Positive Mental Attitude and is a philosophy that I learned when I was five years old.

Chapter 2 How you would describe yourself in one word? Real responses and experiences are shared and explored in this chapter.

Chapter 3 What is your motto? It's important we all have our own motto and I will tell you why.

Chapter 4 What your most valuable possession? Our most valuable possessions are not necessarily material possessions.

Chapter 5 Love is the most powerful gift that we have and we all need love in our lives in order to have a positive mindset.

Chapter 6 This chapter is all about time management to keep you on a positive track. Achieving our goals and tasks is one of the best ways to feel positive and accomplished. If you can increase your productivity you can keep and maintain your positive mindset.

Chapter 7 Priorities, one of the most important journeys in life is learning about what is truly important and what isn't.

Chapter 8 Seven steps to a Positive Mental Attitude. Increasing positive thinking is key and I break it down into seven steps to help you increase your Positive Mental Attitude.

Chapter 9 Addresses five habits to maintain your Positive Mental Mindset.

Chapter 10 Practice makes perfect. By this chapter you have seen multiple techniques to develop and increase your positive mindset. In this final chapter I will cover how you can practice techniques to continue your growth.

I hope that this book helps you in your journey to develop and increase your positive mindset. My philosophy in anything I do in life, whether it's teaching, giving motivational seminars, and writing and coaching, is to have the power of one. The power of one is my goal to help at least one person. I hope that person is you.

Coaching Offer

Are you looking for a book publishing coach to help with turning your potential book into a bestseller?

Contact Paul today at Brodie@BrodieConsultingGroup.com to set up a free call.

Did you know that coaching fees are often tax deductible for people who use coaching to improve business and professional skills? Check with your accountant for details.

Coaching is one of the best investments that you can make for your future success.

Chapter 1 What is PMA?

"When you discover your mission, you will feel its demand. It will fill you with enthusiasm and a burning desire to get to work on it." W. Clement Stone

I created the PMA seminar in September 2008. It was the first seminar that I created and the first thing I realized was that I would need to educate my audience on what PMA meant. PMA is short for Positive Mental Attitude and is a philosophy that I learned when I was about five years old.

One of the main pioneers of PMA is the late W. Clement Stone. He was the President of Combined Insurance and lived by the philosophy of having a positive mental attitude and emphasized the power of thinking positive. Both my parents worked for Combined Insurance when I was growing up.

During company events they would always have motivational talks that were given to the insurance sales force. The company was very family oriented and I was allowed to attend events. The main questions asked during the conferences was "How is your PMA?" and "How do you feel?"

The answer to both questions was that you felt healthy, happy, and terrific. You typically yelled the answer so that everyone at the conference could hear that you felt healthy, happy, and terrific. I remember one sales conference in particular that was held in Corpus Christi, Texas. My dad decided to have some fun and to call me out when he was doing one of his motivational talks at the conference by bringing me to the main stage.

There were probably 200-300 people at the conference and my dad wanted me to do the PMA yell with feeling healthy, happy, and terrific. My dad loved to put me on the spot, but as a fairly introverted seven-year-old at the time. I was having none of it. I went to the stage, but was not going to do the yell in front of the entire conference!

I proceeded to stare at him and tell him that I was not going to do the yell. My mom was furious at my dad, but he did think quickly and came up with another question. He had an employee, Neil, who I did not like. He was previously at a sales party at our home a few months prior and thought it would be funny to play a prank on me by pulling me by the ear and trying to drag me around the house. This did not go over well with me. I had to be held back by others because I was ready to defend myself.

My dad, remembering what happened at the party, asked me at the conference what I would say to Neil if he was not producing for a long period of time. I then looked at Neil and pointed at him and said "You're fired". The audience hooted and hollered, it got a huge laugh. However, Neil was not exactly the most popular person after that because most of the crowd ended up hearing the story about what happened at the party.

Another happening at both sales conferences and sales meetings was singing songs. There were multiple songs they sang, the most popular being "If you're happy and you know it clap your hands". Adults would sing the song in unison and would laugh and feel great. It was a great way to improve positive thinking by acting a little goofy and laughing together.

I always enjoyed the conferences. It was always fun and entertaining watching adults singing songs and doing the PMA yell. The main takeaway for me was that everyone was positive, happy, and enjoyed their careers. Mr. Stone was a very smart man. He always linked happiness and positive thinking with more productive and happy employees. The concepts that I learned then have stayed with me throughout my life. They taught me great lessons that I have been able to implement in my books and seminars to help others.

Ask yourself the following questions:

Have you ever sung a song in front of a crowd?

Are you willing to yell that you feel healthy, happy, and terrific?

Has someone ever put you on the spot and how did you react?

Chapter 2 Describe Yourself in One Word

"There are three things extremely hard: steel, a diamond, and to know one's self." Benjamin Franklin

I know this sounds like a difficult challenge, but it will be very helpful to know yourself. We must first get to know ourselves and secondly, must love ourselves if we are going to improve our positive thinking and overall happiness.

When I approach this segment in my PMA seminar it is done in two parts. The first part asks the audience to describe themselves in one word. Usually, I end up having two to four volunteers and their answers range from happy, funny, sleepy, dopey (yes someone actually said that), whiny (honesty is always a plus), fearful, caring, and many other words. This exercise always gets the audience thinking.

After this segment I show a slide about how I describe myself in one word. The word I start with is caring and then add several more including entertaining, logical, witty, stubborn, fun as examples. The point of the exercise is that one word is not enough to describe yourself, but many words help describe who you are to yourself.

For the second part I ask the audience if they would be willing to share what they think others would say about them in one word. This appears to be the most challenging part of the exercise. Several audience members tend to get a little nervous about this exercise. To alleviate their concerns, I offer to serve as an example.

I explain to my audience that I actually do this exercise not only with family and good friends, but people I'm not particularly close with. At that point, I show a slide that has a wide range of words including the following: entertaining, logical, analytical, caring, vocal, leader, inspirational, polarizing, son, educator, musical, brother, type-a, impulsive, loyal, goofy, sensitive, rebel, driven, and perfectionist.

This example sets the audience at ease and after showing the example invites volunteers to share what they felt that their friends, family, and acquaintances would say about them. Words range from smart, sassy, angry, sad, boring, pretty, silly, passionate, introvert, taskmaster, controlling.

The responses cause reactions ranging from laughs, awes, and even some silent responses. The point of the exercise is to get the audience to focus on themselves and to help discover who they believe they are and also what they believe others think of them.

In my seminars, I have always made clear that our own perceptions are all that matter at the end of the day. We do this exercise in the interest of self-discovery, but my goal is for the audience to see both perspectives.

Ask yourself the following questions:

Have you ever attempted to describe yourself in one word?

Are you willing ask others to describe yourself in one word?

Are you open to seeing both perspectives?

Chapter 3 What is Your Motto

"I have a motto: Work to become, not to acquire." Alan Kulwicki

After I cover the first segment about word description, the next area is about mottos. Most of my friends have a motto they live by. For me, it took many years to discover what I felt was the perfect motto for myself.

After hearing the responses shared by the audience, I introduce my motto, which is Veritas et Utilitas. It is Latin and translates to Truth and service or truth and helpfulness depending on the translation. This is also the motto of Howard University. I feel it is what describes me best.

Truth, I tend to be very direct and even blunt at times. My friends always know where I stand on things. I don't like to play games or be dishonest. Service, or helpfulness, describes my philosophy in life to always make every effort to give back and to others. Whether that is as an author helping my readership on their personal journey, as a teacher helping my students, or as a volunteer with the Texas Special Olympics, it is my philosophy to give back and serve others. I feel we are all servant leaders.

I view mottos as the modern day mission statement. A motto can describe not only yourself, but also your goals in life. Hopefully your goals help not only yourself become successful in life, but also help others too. Whether it is as an educator, author, maintenance person, custodian, mailman, salesman, musician, or any other field, we are all here to help one another.

Ask yourself the following questions:

What is your motto?

Are you willing to create your own motto if you do not have one?

Do you feel that your motto describes what you want to accomplish in life?

Chapter 4 Most Valuable Possession

"Time is at once the most valuable and the most perishable of all our possessions." John Randolph

One of the most thought provoking questions that I pose during my seminars is "What is your most valuable possession?" This elicits a lot of responses and can be quite emotional. I remember giving the PMA seminar in Newport Beach, California at a leadership conference in 2009. One of the members of the audience was a good friend and mentor of mine. He was a college professor at the time and shared with the audience what his most valuable possession was.

The possession most valuable to him was a piece of jewelry that his father had passed on to him. At that point, he broke down into tears because this piece of jewelry was all he had left to remember his father and explained how he always wore it wherever he went.

His story was not about the material possession, but the significance of what it meant to him because it belonged to someone he cared so deeply for. I had another member of the audience that day say the most important possession to them was time because it was something that you could never get back.

At other PMA seminars responses have ranged from family, cell phones, one's mind, love of an organization, education, passion for life, music, and pets.

In my view, our most valuable possessions are time and memories. Time, as previously mentioned, is definitely something that we can never get back. As you get older you realize just how precious time is. I chose memories as well because they become a part of us for our entire lives.

Most people tend to view possessions materialistically. In The Pursuit of Happiness, I detailed my philosophy about money and why family and friends are more important than money ever will be. As someone who has both had money and lived below the poverty line, I have learned that time and memories are what is important. Spending that time with the people that you love and care about is crucial. In the next chapter we will go into more detail about the power of love in our lives.

Ask yourself the following questions:

What is your most valuable possession?

Why is it your most valuable possession?

Is your most valuable possession a material one?

Chapter 5 The Power of Love

"In our imaginations we believe that love is apart from us. Actually there is nothing but love, once we are ready to accept it. When you truly find love, you find yourself." Deepak Chopra

In chapter 5 of The Pursuit of Happiness I reference one of my favorite movies. The movie is called Love Actually. I started the chapter with the following quote:

> *"Whenever I get gloomy with the state of the world, I think about the arrivals gate at Heathrow Airport. General opinion's starting to make out that we live in a world of hatred and greed, but I don't see that. It seems to be that love is everywhere. Often, it's not particularly dignified or newsworthy, but it's always there – fathers and sons, mothers and daughters, husbands and wives, boyfriends, girlfriends, old friends. When the planes hit the Twin Towers, as far as I know, none of the phone calls from the people on board were messages of hate or revenge – they were all messages of love. If you look for it, I've got a sneaky feeling you'll find that love actually is all around." Prime Minister (Hugh Grant's Character) in Love Actually*

The quote is a reminder that love is all around us. In our battle to remain positive and pursue our own happiness, one of the greatest reminders is to use love instead of hate. Love in truly does conquer all in my opinion. It has taken me many years to realize that.

There were times in my past when I did not always feel love. Growing up I struggled a lot with anger and depression. Depression is still the biggest challenges that I have, but I have been able to release the anger I had through both love and forgiveness.

The relationship with my dad was a prime example. In The Pursuit of Happiness I went into great detail about that relationship. To sum it up, I learned to forgive the past of him abandoning both myself and my mom. Due to that forgiveness I was able to build a very good relationship with him in recent years. It was not easy, but the past is the past, and cannot be changed. We do have the ability to change both the present and the future. Having this mentality has allowed me to move on from the past hurt.

I know that the time that I have left with my dad is not going to be long. He is in his seventies and has previous health issues that have severely impacted his long term health. Fortunately, he made the choice many years ago to give up his vices and he is definitely a much better person now than he was.

It is much better to focus on love instead of hate and the baggage of your past. Do you use baggage to drag you down or do you use baggage to motivate you?

I ask this because in order to focus on being positive, we must use the baggage of the past as motivation for ourselves. Through that motivation we can focus on love instead of hate and anger. To paraphrase Yoda in Star Wars, anger leads to hate and hate leads to suffering. There is no point in hating another person and especially yourself.

In my experience, forgiveness leads to living a more positive and happy life and thus leads to loving yourself. If you do not love yourself then how can you expect to give and receive love to and from others? Our relationships with our family, friends, significant others, all rely on love. To reference Love Actually, "Love actually is all around."

Ask yourself the following questions:

Do you currently hate another person or even yourself?

Are you willing to give up hate for love?

Will you forgive people who have hurt you to move on?

Chapter 6 Time Management

"Money is not the prime asset in life, time is." Gordon Gekko (as played by Michael Douglas in the movie Wall Street)

One of the main questions I am asked is how in the world have I have managed to write and publish seven bestselling books while working full time as a Special Education Teacher...

Without proper time management there would be no way that I could do both in addition to public speaking at conferences and campuses and also coaching my clients. Time management is a must in order to be successful and maintain a positive outlook.

One of the biggest challenges to achieve our goals in life is procrastination. In Just Do It I wrote about how I had to manage my time very carefully when I started to teach. At the time, I was in my first year teaching and running two ESL (English as a Second Language) programs at two junior high schools. I was already stretched thin, but the opportunity was too great to pass up. The program, as it was new to the university, offered an incredible deal where I could get my master's degree for only five thousand dollars.

I decided to take the risk and started by completing and submitting all of the paperwork and essays. It was still an application based process and the paperwork would take a while as the school wanted me to write multiple essays with subjects including my philosophy of teaching and what influenced me to become a teacher.

Overall, I had five essays to write aside from needing to submit multiple applications that would require transcripts, teacher samples, and other files. The process took me over two weeks to get everything ready, but I got it done. It was a great feeling to complete everything and to get it sent out.

One of the most important aspects of achieving your goals is to show up, take the first step, take another step, and keep going. What I have found with goal setting is if you can start the process and keep taking those steps and work hard, then anything is possible.

I found out several weeks later that the university was very pleased with the paperwork that I turned in and I was accepted to the program. It was not easy even with the content being online. I was required to film several of my classes and lessons that I taught. It was very rigorous, but well worth it. Going through the program made me a better teacher and I received an additional teacher stipend for having the master's degree, which has already paid for the cost of the degree.

Without making time management a top priority, there is no way that I could have gotten through graduate school while working full time as a teacher. I made it a point to budget my day so there would be time to get all my work done and still have time to relax.

As an author I tend to do most of my writing on the weekends or during holidays over summer. During my first year writing books I did some writing during the regular work week, but learned over time the best way to write and teach was to keep them separate and focus on one task at a time.

I am actually writing this book during the holiday break. You must find time for yourself after a long day of work. One thing I have done is to complete other parts of my business from coaching, marketing, branding etc. in the evening. The actual writing of my books I specifically set time aside for days I do not teach so I can create the best possible books for my readership.

With this approach I feel it is the best way to manage time so if you do have a second business or other goals then definitely plan them out. Focus on certain aspects of your second business during the weekday after getting home for work, but try to not dedicate more than two to three hours each night as you do not want to burn out.

You also want to make time for your family, friends, and even an hour or two to just relax and do whatever makes you happy. One area I am making more a priority is both meditation and mindfulness. Meditation can be as simple as focusing on one object in a room and just looking at that while attempting to clear out any other thoughts.

As an example, in my bedroom I have canvases and photography from my trips to Maui over the past fourteen years. There is one picture in particular that I focus on. It is a picture of the view from the balcony of the condo where I stayed at last year. It is one of my favorite views and I had the picture printed out, enlarged, and framed. When I really want to focus and clear out my mind I focus only on that picture.

I feel with the right game plan, focus, and time to relax, you will be able to accomplish what you want. This great sense of accomplishment will not only help you achieve a positive mindset, but can help you to continue to maintain your positive mindset over time.

Ask yourself the following questions:

Are you able to maximize your time?

Is time management a challenge for you?

Are you willing to try meditation?

Chapter 7 Priorities

"To succeed today, you have to set priorities, decide what you stand for." Lee Iacocca

What are your priorities? What is important to you?

Those are two questions that will define not only what is important in your life, but also how it shapes your positive mindset. We must strive to know who we are and where we are going. If we know those two things and have a positive mindset, then there is nothing you can't accomplish.

For me, I knew very early in life that my family would be my priority. In The Pursuit of Happiness I covered some of my struggles growing up and what I wanted to do in order to be able to take care of my mom as she got older. In 1992, at seventeen years old, I had the opportunity to work at the same marketing research company as my mother. I worked at the company for the next 13 years and was promoted multiple times. By 2001, I was the assistant manager and my mom was the branch manager. The part that made me proudest was that my mom never hired me or gave me any promotions. All of the promotions were through her bosses. She was very tough on me and for that I am exponentially grateful.

From 1994 to 2005 I worked my way through college. It was a tough grind, but ten years later I finally graduated. During New Year's Eve 2004 I told my mom how much I really appreciated all that she has done for me over the years and that I had a plan. Within two months we would get a house and that within a few years I would be able to take care of the bills so that she would be able to retire.

On February 1, 2005, we moved in to the dream home that we still have today. We were able to find the perfect home. The price was very fair and with our two incomes, we were already approved for the financing. Mom was getting close to retirement and I did not want her living in a town house because she always dreamed of having her own home again. I knew that I could make it happen.

Money does not buy happiness, but if used correctly can enhance your life. I knew that I would be making more money after graduation and as my income would rise my mom's income would decrease.

Another curveball was that the market research company that we worked at was being sold. We met with the president of the company and he was straight forward about the sale. He had another position for my mom, but he would not have a local position for me. In this situation some people might get angry or bitter, instead I thanked him for that entire experience and explained that I appreciated the opportunity to work for him. At that point, I shook his hand to express my gratitude and thanked him for having a position available for my mom.

During this time, I wanted to start a mediation company. I had gone through several trainings and was certified to do mediations. Unfortunately, most of the business was given to attorneys at law firms and it was going to be a tough road ahead to have a sustainable full time career in mediation.

In August 2005, I started my journey at Enterprise rent-a-car. I stayed with the company until 2007 and then went into nurse recruiting before finally taking the leap of faith and starting my teaching career, where I have remained ever since.

During that timeframe my mom left market research and returned to selling insurance. Ironically, she went back to Combined Insurance and worked there for several years before finally retiring in 2011. With teaching I was able to take care of the bills and my projections worked out very well. I also started BrodieEDU in 2010 and was already generating revenue through creating an after school program for low cost housing in Kentucky.

My income was in good shape and I was able to have the honor of taking care of family that took such great care of me over the years. I know that not everyone would or could do that for their family. Everyone's situation is different and at times those decisions are due to money. I am very proud to be in a situation where I have the opportunity to support my family and to also pursue my happiness as both a teacher and author.

Everyone has different priorities in life. In my view it comes down to faith, family & friends, and career. With those three things, in addition to the correct mindset, we can accomplish anything that we want to.

Ask yourself the following questions:

What are your priorities?

What is important to you?

Chapter 8 Seven Steps to a Positive Mental Attitude

"Having a positive mental attitude is asking how something can be done rather than saying it can't be done." Bo Bennett

There are multiple steps to developing a positive mental attitude. In this chapter I am going to cover seven steps that will help you along the way.

Step 1 is think positive. Choosing to be positive is the first commitment that you must make in your journey to a positive mental attitude.

Step 2 is to develop a can do attitude. My philosophy with problem solving is that there is always a solution, all you have to do is find it. Focus on the solution instead of just the problem.

Step 3 is do not complain. There will always be challenges in life and complaining about them does not help. There is a fine line between complaining and venting. Venting can be a release, but complaining will hurt in your journey to stay positive.

Step 4 is keep positive thinking friends. You are a product of the people you surround yourself with. In Positivity Attracts I dedicate a chapter to the circle of trust. Having your own circle of trust of family and close friends is a critical element to being and staying positive.

Step 5 is be appreciative. One thing I suggest in particular is creating a gratitude list and one of the most important things that I have learned over the past several years is to express gratitude. Every morning I think of five things that I am grateful for.

This is my gratitude list

1. My family having good health
2. My friends
3. My home
4. My career
5. My choice to be happy every morning

Every time that I think of my gratitude list it makes me happy because my family had good health for the most part, my friends are amazing and happy, I am blessed to have a dream home, I love being a teacher, and I get to drive my dream car daily.

Step 6 is control your frustration. One of the best outlets for this step is to focus on what you can control versus what you cannot control in your life. If you focus on what you can control and you will be the master of your own universe.

Step 7 is live in the present. There is no point in worrying about the past or the future. The best way to develop a positive mindset is to focus on the present and what is in front of you.

Ask yourself the following questions:

Do you struggle to think positive at times?

Are you willing to follow these seven steps in your journey to develop your positive mental attitude?

Do you have a circle of trust?

Chapter 9 Five Habits to Maintain a Positive Mental Attitude

"There is little difference in people, but that little difference makes a big difference. The little difference is attitude. The big difference is whether it is positive or negative." W. Clement Stone

The first habit is to accept whatever situation you find yourself. No situation is ever going to be perfect. You must accept the situation and then work on finding a solution. When I chose to leave the corporate world I was miserable in my job. I was making great money, but felt like a mercenary. I felt that I was not giving back by helping other employees and training them, similar to my previous job at Enterprise. I chose to accept that I would need to make changes career wise and knew that while it was a risk to leave full time employment and a very lucrative career, it was the right decision.

The second habit is to focus on the positive side of each problem. I prefer to focus on the bright side because it is much better to focus on what you can gain instead of what you are losing. Not only does it inspire creativity, but also problem solving to create a positive mindset. When I left the corporate world roughly ten years ago, I was relieved because I knew that I would find something even better as a career path and was not worried at all about the future. The positive side was that I knew that I would find something that I loved and would work less hours with a shorter work commute. The most important positive aspect that I focused on was the realization that my next career would be on my terms and that I would find something meaningful that would allow me to give back to the community.

The third habit is to focus on the solution. My view on issues like this is that there is always a solution, all you have to do is find it. What I realized was that I needed to focus on what was next for me at the time. The solution was to become a teacher. It was not easy as I would need to take certifications, exams, and go through an alternate certification course. I knew it would be hard work, but well worth the new journey and career path.

The fourth habit is to make a list of possible solutions to the problem. In every book that I have written, I have always suggested making lists. The lists range from a gratitude journal, a list for all of the positive things that are happening in life, to both motivational lists and positive thinking lists. The same rings true for creating a list of solutions for problems. When I left the corporate world I wrote out a list of solutions for future employment. After a few weeks of working on the list, everything on the list led me to pursue a career in teaching and was one of the best decisions I ever made. Always focus on the solution and not only the problem.

The fifth habit is to focus on the future. My suggestion for this is to focus on what you want to happen goal wise during the next five to ten years. During that time I knew that going into teaching was not going to be just for a few years. My focus was to teach from ten to thirty years depending on where my career was going. I also figured during that time I would most likely go back to school and get a Master's Degree in Education, which I did. During that time I also realized that my path beyond teaching would be either consulting or doing public speaking. Ten years later that path looks pretty accurate.

Ask yourself the following questions:

Are you willing to accept whatever situation that you find yourself in?

Will you choose to focus on the positive side of the problem?

Are you open to focusing on the solution instead of the problem?

Do you make lists to focus on solving problems?

What will you do to focus on the future?

Chapter 10 Practice Makes Perfect

"Practice makes perfect. After a long time of practicing, our work will become natural, skillful, swift, and steady." Bruce Lee

Over the past nine chapters we have focused on multiple ways to develop and increase your positive mindset. Now that you have the tools in this book, I want to give one more step in this process.

Practice makes perfect. You have heard that expression from many people including the quote above from Bruce Lee. With the tools from this book, the best advice I can give you is to constantly focus on the positive aspects in your own life.

It is not easy to choose to be positive, but it is a choice. In Positivity Attracts I dedicated a chapter with the sole focus on delegating your fears and worries. There are two parts to help delegate your fears and worries. The first part is to delegate your fears and worries to a higher power. I know this is not for everyone, but it has worked for me and for many others. As previously mentioned, I have always believed that we are all on a path and that everything does happen for reason. I believe that by delegating your worries to a higher power, your fears and worries will significantly decrease. You will feel more at peace with yourself.

The second part is to focus on each day one at a time. This can be hard. The way I see it, it's similar to going to see a movie. Before the movie starts there are always trailers for upcoming movies. Instead of focusing on the movie you want to see, you begin thinking about the other movies that are coming out that you hope to see.

Practice makes perfect. With focusing on the positive and what is good in your life, your perspective will become more positive.

In Just Do It I dedicated a chapter specifically towards fighting against adversity. We are all going to have to fight through adversity in a variety of situations. They can be health scares, job changes, family issues, battles with weight, fighting depression, etc. I have had all of those challenges throughout this year and most of my life.

Life is not easy and you have to build a warriors mentality. You also have to realize that as I have mentioned in my previous books, the only perception that matters is your own. No one's perception matters because at the end of the day, what you think is most important.

Again, practice makes perfect. Focus on what you have and how great your life is and your life will change for the better. As someone who fights depression on a daily basis, I can tell you from my own personal battles that exercising your mind to focus on the positive aspects is life changing.

Ask yourself the following questions:

Are you willing to focus on the positive aspects of life by practicing gratitude every day?

Will you choose to focus on the positive things in your life?

Are you open to focusing on what you have in life versus what you do not have?

Conclusion

Through the past ten chapters we have covered a range of topics from what is PMA and describing yourself in one word and mottos, to utilizing time management and focusing on our priorities. In addition, we have also covered seven steps to a positive mental attitude and five habits to maintain a positive mental attitude. My hope is that this book will help with your own personal quest to develop and increase your positive mindset.

I want to thank you for reading my eighth book. Writing each book is a labor of love. I write about things I am passionate about and I believe having a happy, positive and motivated mindset is one of the most important things in life.

Stayed tuned for the release of my next self-help book, Be Your Greatest Champion and I invite you to check out Eat Less and Move More, Motivation 101, The Pursuit of Happiness, Positivity Attracts, Maui, Just Do It and Book Publishing for Beginners.

More Books by Paul

"Quick and inexpensive reads for self-improvement, a healthier lifestyle, and book publishing"

Seven time Amazon bestselling author, Paul Brodie believes that books should be inexpensive, straightforward, direct, and not have a bunch of fluff.

Each of his books were created to solve problems including living a healthy lifestyle, increasing motivation, improving positive thinking, and how to help authors publish and market their books.

What makes Paul's books different is his ability to explain complex ideas and strategies in a simple, accessible way that you can implement immediately.

Want to know more?

Go to www.BrodieEDU.com/Books

Author Resource Guide

Do you want to publish your first book?

Are you an author who is looking to grow your business and increase revenue?

In my fourth book, Book Publishing for Beginners, I offered a free guide that includes step-by-step instructions to help with recording your audiobook, how to upload your Kindle book to Amazon, and how to convert your Kindle eBook to paperback. I also provide examples of sales copy to help with book sales, how to use HTML in your book description, and how to utilize different back end products to offer your readership.

In addition, the guide includes contact information for my own personal editor and my book designer who can create a great book cover for as low as ten dollars. The first chapter of my next publishing book, Book Publishing for Authors is also offered in the guide.

I want to offer this free guide to assist in your journey of writing and publishing your own book. It is highly recommended that you also check out my Book Publishing for Beginners book as it will definitely help in your journey.

Go to www.BrodieEDU.com/resources to download the free resource guide.

About the Author

Paul Brodie is the President of BrodieEDU, an education consulting firm that specializes in the development of literacy programs, motivational seminars for universities and corporations, and wellness education. He is also the CEO of Brodie Consulting Group, which specializes in coaching clients with publishing their own books and advising clients on branding, marketing, self-improvement and personal development.

Brodie also serves as a Special Education Teacher for the Fort Worth Independent School District. Previously Paul taught Special Education from 2014-2016 for the Hurst-Euless-Bedford Independent School District.

From 2011-2014, Brodie served as a Grant Coordinator for the ASPIRE program in the Birdville Independent School District. As coordinator, he created instructional and enrichment programming for over 800 students and 100 parents in the ASPIRE before and after school programs. He also served for many years on the Board of Directors for the Leadership Development Council, Inc. with leading the implementation of educational programming in low cost housing.

Previously, Brodie spent many years in the corporate world and decided to leave a lucrative career in the medical field to follow his passion and transitioned into education. From 2008 to 2011, he was a highly successful teacher in Arlington, TX where he taught English as a Second Language. Brodie turned a once struggling ESL program into one of the top programs in the school district. Many of his students have moved on to journalism, AVID, art classes, and a number of the students exited the ESL program entirely.

His methods included music, movies, graphic novels, and many high engagement methods including using technology, games, cultural celebrations, and getting parents involved in their children's education. Brodie's approach has been called unconventional but highly effective, revolutionary, and highly engaging.

Brodie earned an M.A. in Teaching from Louisiana College and B.B.A. in Management from the University of Texas at Arlington. Brodie is a bestselling author and has written seven books. He wrote his first book, Eat Less and Move More: My Journey in the summer of 2015. Brodie's goal of the book was to help those like himself who have had challenges with weight. The goal of his first book was to promote not only weight loss but also health and wellness. He is also the author of Motivation 101, Positivity Attracts, Book Publishing for Beginners, The Pursuit of Happiness, Just Do It and Maui. All seven books are Amazon bestsellers and are based on his motivational seminars, book publishing, and struggles with weight.

His motivational seminars have been featured at multiple universities and at leadership conferences across the United States since 2005. Brodie is active in professional organizations and within the community and currently serves on the

Advisory Board for Advent Urban Youth Development and as a volunteer with the Special Olympics. He continues to be involved with The International Business Fraternity of Delta Sigma Pi and has served in many positions since 2002 including National Vice President – Organizational Development, Leadership Foundation Trustee, National Organizational Development Chair, District Director, and in many other volunteer leadership roles. He resides in Arlington, TX.

Acknowledgments

Thank you to God for guidance and protection throughout my life.

Thank YOU the reader for investing your time reading this book.

Thank you to my amazing mom, Barbara Brodie for all of the years of support and a kick in the butt when needed.

Thank you to Schreese Fontaine for writing the foreword for this book. I have greatly appreciated my adopted little sister's friendship and support for the past eleven years.

Thank you to my awesome sister, Dr. Heather Ottaway for all of the help and feedback with my books and also with my motivational seminars. It is scary how similar we are.

Thank you to Devin Mooneyham for serving as the editor of my eighth book. The slicing and dicing as always was very much appreciated and I could not have gotten this book published without her assistance. I also want to congratulate Devin on the upcoming birth of her first child, Livia Mooneyham.

Thank you to Lindsay Palmer who is working tirelessly to get me booked on college campuses for seminars throughout the United States. I could not have a better team of people to work with on Team Brodie.

Thank you to all who have served on the BrodieEDU Advisory Board.

Thank you to my dad, Bill "The Wild Scotsman" Brodie for his encouragement and support with the business aspects of BrodieEDU and Brodie Consulting Group.

Thank you to Shannon and Robert Winckel (two members of the four horsemen with myself and our good friend, Derrada Rubell-Asbell) for their friendship and support. Shannon and Robert are two of my best teacher friends and are always great sounding boards for ideas.

Thank you to (Don) Omar Sandoval for his friendship and help with several BrodieEDU projects including building our awesome website.

Thank you to all of the amazing friends that I have worked with over the past twenty plus years. Each of them has made a great impact on my life.

Thank you to all of my students that I have had the honor to teach over the years. I am very proud of each of my kids.

Thank you to Delta Sigma Pi Business Fraternity. I learned a great deal about public speaking and leadership through the organization and every experience that I have had helped me become the person that I am today.

Thank you to my three best friends: J. Dean Craig, Jen Mamber, and Aaron Krzycki. We have gone through a lot together and I look forward to many more years of friendship.

Thank you to all of the students past and present at the UT Arlington and UT Austin chapters of DSP. Both schools mean a lot to me and I look forward to seeing them again at some point in the near future.

Thank you to the Lott Family (Stacy, Kerry, Lexi, and Austin) for their friendship over the past seven years.

Thank you to Robin Clites for always taking care of things at the house with ensuring that Mom and I can always get that family vacation every year.

Contact Information

Go to www.YouTube.com/BrodieEDU to see why you should consider booking Paul for seminars, coaching, or consulting.

Paul can be reached at Brodie@BrodieConsultingGroup.com

Website www.BrodieEDU.com

Check out all of Paul's books at www.brodieedu.com/books/

@BrodieEDU on Twitter

Paul G. Brodie author page on Facebook

Paul G. Brodie author page on Amazon

BrodieEDU Facebook Page

BrodieEDU YouTube Channel

Quotes

I wanted to share with you the quotes that I used to start each chapter of PMA: Positive Mental Attitude.

Enjoy,

Paul

Chapter 1 What is PMA?

"When you discover your mission, you will feel its demand. It will fill you with enthusiasm and a burning desire to get to work on it." W. Clement Stone

Chapter 2 Describe Yourself in One Word

"There are three things extremely hard: steel, a diamond, and to know one's self." Benjamin Franklin

Chapter 3 What is Your Motto

"I have a motto: Work to become, not to acquire." Alan Kulwicki

Chapter 4 Most Valuable Possession

"Time is at once the most valuable and the most perishable of all our possessions." John Randolph

Chapter 5 The Power of Love

"In our imaginations we believe that love is apart from us. Actually there is nothing but love, once we are ready to accept it. When you truly find love, you find yourself." Deepak Chopra

Chapter 6 Time Management

"Money is not the prime asset in life, time is." Gordon Gekko (as played by Michael Douglas in the movie Wall Street)

Chapter 7 Priorities

"To succeed today, you have to set priorities, decide what you stand for." Lee Iacocca

Chapter 8 Seven Steps to a Positive Mental Attitude

"Having a positive mental attitude is asking how something can be done rather than saying it can't be done." Bo Bennett

Chapter 9 Five Habits to Maintain a Positive Mental Attitude

"There is little difference in people, but that little difference makes a big difference. The little difference is attitude. The big difference is whether it is positive or negative." W. Clement Stone

Chapter 10 Practice Makes Perfect

"Practice makes perfect. After a long time of practicing, our work will become natural, skillful, swift, and steady." Bruce Lee

Feedback

Please leave a review for my book as I would greatly appreciate your feedback.

I also welcome you to contact me with any suggestions at Brodie@BrodieConsultingGroup.com